The PRAYER
that Changed My Life
God is Good All the Time

NAN A. WEAVER

Copyright © 2017 by Nan A. Weaver

The Prayer that Changed My Life
God is Good All the Time
by Nan A. Weaver

Printed in the United States of America.
Edited by Xulon Press.

ISBN 9781498494441

All rights reserved solely by the author. The author guarantees all contents are original and do not infringe upon the legal rights of any other person or work. No part of this book may be reproduced in any form without the permission of the author. The views expressed in this book are not necessarily those of the publisher.

Unless otherwise indicated, Scripture quotations taken from the Holy Bible, New International Version (NIV). Copyright © 2011 by Zondervan. Used by permission. All rights reserved

www.xulonpress.com

Table of Contents

Introduction vii
Chapter 1 – My Early Years. 13
Chapter 2 – Out of the Nest. 19
Chapter 3 – Strengthening My Faith 23
Chapter 4 – A New Chapter of My Life 29
Chapter 5 – My Prayer 39
Chapter 6 – Satan Tried to Defeat but God Showed
    His Love. 43
Chapter 7 – The Answer to My Prayer 67
Chapter 8 – Lessons Learned. 75
Chapter 9–Conclusion. 91

Introduction

This book is not intended for theologians or for people who want to dig deeper into the Bible, but rather for those who have been hurt, or have had to deal with the "whys" of a tragedy and are searching for a deeper relationship with God. We live in a sin-cursed world where there is suffering all around us, and yet I have always been told God is a good God. Can I count on Him when times get tough? What does it mean when someone says, "God is only a prayer away"? Does it mean I simply have to tell Him my troubles and He will be a genie in a bottle and make all my hurts and disappointments disappear? If they don't go away, does that mean He did not hear me or has decided I am on my own?

God has always been good to me, but I began to sense that He was like my "Santa Claus." When I had a problem, He was required to fix it because, after all, He is a good God and that is what He does. I was okay when He did not fix all my problems, because I had my wonderful husband, who always had a way of working out my problems. However, there are millions of people who face difficult challenges every day. Why isn't God good to them—or is He?

In January 2015, I told God that I had a deep desire to know Him better. I wanted to understand His character so that I could learn how to trust Him in all areas of my life. This book tells how Satan tried to use a tragedy to turn me away from God, and how God used it to answer my prayer. It also shares the awesome lessons He has taught me since the tragedy.

I have spent the past year and a half searching Scriptures and reading books by godly men and women to learn how to have a closer relationship with the God of the universe. When my husband of forty-six years, who was my everything, died, I was lost. My Christian life to this point was more about religion than a relationship with God. Although I can quote my fair share of Bible verses, and I taught Sunday school for many years, I never bothered to get to know God's character and who He is to *me*. The sad part is He always wanted to be my everything, but I pushed Him aside and went to Him only in the "911" times of my life. The Lord is such a gentleman, and He never forces Himself on us, but as the Bible says,

Introduction

"Come near to God and he will come near to you" (James 4:8). We just need to take that first step.

My new life's journey with God is just beginning, and it is comforting to know that His character never changes, which means He is the same yesterday, today, and forever. This assures me that the same God who was by my side at a desperate time of my life is right here with me today, leading me as I seek His guidance. I look forward to all that He has in store for me. I can testify that our tragedies are His opportunities to show us great things that we can't conceive of, *if* we yield to His plans that He has for us.

I trust that, if you are a believer in Christ and do not have that close personal relationship with God, after reading this book, you will have a desire to seek to know Him better. If you are not a Christ follower, I pray this book will direct you to Christ, who loves you so much that He took your sins to the cross so that you too can have a relationship with God that outshines anything that you can imagine.

Dedication

To my husband and best friend of over forty-six years, Tyre, who was promoted to heaven on April 13, 2015.

WAR EAGLE!

CHAPTER 1
MY EARLY YEARS

My dad was an air force officer, and my mom stayed home with my brother, my two younger sisters, and me. Each day before dad arrived home from work, Mom always changed to a clean ironed dress, brushed her hair, and put on red lipstick. Their love for each other was so evident, and Mom always wanted to look her best for Dad. I never recall hearing them argue. They both demonstrated the love of Christ to each other and to each of us kids.

My parents loved the Lord and desired for their children to grow up knowing Him. Sunday was the Lord's day, so we attended Sunday school and church each Sunday morning and returned to church on Sunday evening. There was never a question of whether or not we went to church; it was a given in our household! Being a military family, we moved a lot, but at each duty station, we always found a Bible-based church.

Dad usually ended up serving on the deacon board, teaching Sunday school classes, and preaching when asked. He was an intellect, so as a young child, I never understood what he was talking about when he preached about a "sovereign, omnipotent God." I've heard it said that your dad is a picture of what you think God is like. In my case, that was exactly right! Dad was so smart, and he used big words to describe God, so my picture of God was formed early in life as one who was too smart for me to understand. My dad was on such a high pedestal in my book that when we sang "This Is My Father's World," I thought we were singing about Dad. After all, he traveled around the world, so it made sense that the world belonged to him.

My mom taught kindergarten through second graders in Sunday school for as long as I can remember. Mom's love for the children in her classes was evident by the way she greeted them with smiles and hugs, always making each child feel special. She exemplified Jesus's love for people. When I was too old to attend her class, I became her helper so I could hear her tell Bible stories. She made the stories come alive. I loved to hear about Jesus feeding the five thousand, healing people, and being kind to people even when they were not kind to Him. In my eyes, there was such a contrast between God and Jesus. To me, God was the intellectual for older people who understood Him, and Jesus was the compassionate Savior who I as a child related to.

When I was in fourth grade, a friend and I attended a church meeting at the local junior high school. I vividly remember the preacher explaining sin, and sharing that the Bible says we are all sinners. He went on to explain that God is a holy God who cannot allow sin where He is in heaven, but that He loves us so much He made a way through His Son, Jesus Christ, to be the Savior of the world. The Holy Spirit spoke to our hearts, and we were the first ones down the aisle at the invitation. A kind lady explained to us how to be saved: we were to admit that we were sinners and missed the mark to get to heaven; believe that God showed His love toward mankind by having His only Son, Jesus Christ, die on the cross for all our sins; confess our sins; and ask Jesus into our lives. We prayed and accepted Jesus Christ as our Savior that night. I remember asking my friend the next day if she felt any different, and we both agreed we didn't, but nobody could tell me I was not saved because the lady who'd led me to the Lord had showed me in God's Word the way to have eternal life, and I believed the Bible was true.

It wasn't until I was a senior in high school that I took the next step of obedience by being baptized. It was time to publicly acknowledge what I had done in fourth grade. My pastor at the time, and a spiritual mentor today, Cal Fox, told me that before being baptized, he would like me to give my testimony. *Me? The girl who was too shy to talk to people in general was not being asked to talk in front of the entire congregation?* Looking back, it was a huge step in my Christian walk. I have no idea what I said, but this was a first step in trusting God to see me through a situation I had never dealt with before, and He was faithful to get me through it.

During this time of my life, while I had a love for the Lord, I struggled with having to go to church when none of my friends attended. They were fine without church, but it wasn't a topic of discussion in our household. As long as I lived under my parents' roof, I attended church each and every Sunday. This became a way of life in our home when I married and had a family of my own.

During the spring of my senior year of high school, my dad came home one day and asked us if we would like to move to Germany for three years. His choice was to retire or to accept one more tour of duty to Germany. It was an easy choice for me because I had just finished taking two years of German, so I could speak the language—or so I thought.

The family agreed to the move, and in September 1967, we moved to Wiesbaden, Germany, and I found myself in for a rude awakening! I could not understand the Germans because they did not speak the German dialect I had learned. Of course, we went to church on base each Sunday, but there were no opportunities where I could meet people my age who spoke English, so I was extremely lonely for the first few months. I wondered if I had made a drastic mistake by voting for this move. I finally managed to find a job at the air force base exchange in the "notions" department, cutting fabric. It was not my choice job, but at least I got out of the house and could communicate with English-speaking people. Looking back, this move was all part of God's plan for my life.

CHAPTER 2

OUT OF THE NEST

It was at the base exchange that I met the love of my life, who was a sergeant in the air force. He was from Alabama—a state I knew nothing about since we had never been stationed in the Deep South. On our first date, he swept me off my feet. He was such a gentleman, and he treated me so special by taking me to his favorite restaurant, where he knew the owner and made sure I was treated like a queen. I went home that night and told my parents, "Tyre even opened the car door for me!" to which my dad replied, "That's what he is supposed to do." Well, I had dated my fair share of guys, and none of them had ever opened the car door for me!

Within five months, we were engaged, and four months later, we were married. I tell everyone I was married twice to the same man. The first time was in Basel, Switzerland, and the second was in Germany. The Germans had so much red tape to jump through to get married in Germany, so our other option was to go to Switzerland, which we did. My parents stood up for us at the courthouse, and then the following weekend we had a church wedding in Germany. As long as we had a legal marriage license, the Germans recognized us as married, so they did not care if we had a church wedding in their country. However, in my mother's eyes, we weren't considered married until we'd said our vows before God, so Mom would not allow me to live with Tyre until after the church wedding. After returning from our honeymoon, we attended church when we were not traveling throughout Europe. Actually, I was glad I didn't *have* to attend church any longer. It had become a ritual in my life, and I didn't see the need for going every single Sunday, unlike Tyre, who'd also grown up attending church, but it had never become a formality like it had been for me. To me, missing church felt like I was skipping school, and I feared God would punish me for not attending church.

Fifteen months later, we said good-bye to my parents in Germany and flew home to Tyre's hometown, LaFayette, Alabama. I was looking forward to meeting his family and being back in the States, where I could understand everyone.

What a shock when Tyre's dad opened his mouth—I couldn't understand a word he said. He had such a thick Southern accent, he could have been speaking German for all I knew. Then I discovered his entire family spoke "Southern." I was pregnant, I still had morning sickness, and I was in *another* strange place with *more* people I could not understand. It was a difficult time in my life.

Tyre worked seven days a week in a manufacturing plant. I was at home by myself, longing for a friend. Now I wanted to go to church, but we only had one car. Looking back, it was the prompting of the Holy Spirit and my parents' training that put the desire in me to go to church. For as long as I could remember, my parents had led by example by taking the family to church on Sundays, and now there was a major void in my life. One day, I learned that one of Tyre's friends attended a local church, so I called and asked if I could go with her and her husband. I don't remember the denomination. It wasn't like the Baptist church I was used to, but I did not care; it was Sunday, and I was in church. Three months later, Lynn was born and church was once again on the back burner.

Over the next several months, I learned the "Southern" language, and I ventured out to talk with Tyre's family without Tyre at my side. I soon became close with his sister, Connie.

It wasn't until after our son, Ty, was born that I felt the need to find a church home so that our children could learn about Jesus. Connie and I found a Baptist church and started attending with our children, and our husbands attended when they weren't working. My Sunday ritual was to get the kids dressed, go to church, and listen to the preaching, and then our Sunday duty was over for another week. The Bible tells not to forsake assembling together (Hebrews 10:25), but when the focus is on a ritual rather than building a relationship with a loving God who is full of grace, we have missed the purpose of church attendance.

After Tyre was laid off at the manufacturing plant, he went to work full-time at the Opelika Police Department and attended Auburn University. Times were hard. We applied for a HUD house, which was for low-income people, but Tyre did not make enough money to qualify! His boss ended up giving him a raise so that we could purchase a HUD house. We thanked God for it, but then we always thanked God when something good happened. After all, that was what you did!

CHAPTER 3
STRENGTHENING MY FAITH

After Tyre graduated from college, we moved around with his job, always attending church, but it wasn't until we attended an independent church in Birmingham, Alabama, that we both surrendered our lives to the Lord and wanted Him to be the head of our home and to direct our lives. It was at this time that the Lord gave Tyre his call to be the spiritual leader of our home: "As for me and my household, we will serve the Lord" (Joshua 24:15b). He took his family to church and made sure his children were involved in youth activities at church.

Two years later, we moved again and started attending another independent church. But rather than building my relationship with God, I was tossed into legalism—keeping

The Prayer that Changed My Life

rules and regulations—completely forgetting Jesus's love and compassion that I had learned about in our former church and in my mother's Sunday school class. One time, I wore capris to drop off something at the church during the week, and I was told that I was not to wear them in church. After that admonishment, I took it so far that I wouldn't go to my mailbox without wearing a skirt. I was in bondage to my focus on pleasing man rather than pleasing God.

In 1984, Tyre felt the Lord leading him to quit his management job. By then, we had four children: Lynn, Ty IV, Bryan, and Katie. I was a homemaker and we were financially comfortable, so for him to tell me he was quitting his job . . . let's just say it sent me over the edge. To top it off, he decided he wanted to start his own business in the Florida Panhandle, which meant no steady income for a while. As a homemaker, I felt fear grip my heart. How would we feed our kids? Where would we live? I remember our son, Bryan, who was three at the time, praying, "Thank you, God, for our house in Pensacola." I thought, *Bless his heart, we don't have a clue where we are going to live.* Little did I know, the Lord would use Bryan's faith to strengthen my faith.

The following weekend, we drove around Pensacola, Florida, looking for a house. One house we saw had a faded "For Rent" sign on the power pole and a moving van in the driveway. I jumped out of the car and asked the people if they were moving in or out. They were a Christian couple moving to Virginia, and they had been praying for renters. All I could do was breathe a prayer, "Forgive me, Lord, for my lack of faith."

We joined a wonderful church where we had great opportunity to grow in the Lord, but my life was so full of wanting to do right so that God would be pleased with me that I was blinded to the truths of the Bible. I knew the Bible verse that said, "My God will meet all your needs according to the riches of his glory in Christ Jesus" (Philippians 4:19), but I wanted to add my good works to His word to be sure He would keep His promise. I am sure the Lord rolls His eyes around when He sees His children *trying* rather than *trusting* in Him to do what He says He will do. I thank Him for His unfailing love. He loves us in spite of our trying to do things on our own.

He was so faithful to us over the years, and His timing was always perfect, like the time the credit card company called and asked when we planned to make a payment. I told them I would have my husband return their call because I had no idea how we were going to pay the bill. Tyre's business hadn't taken off, so money was extremely tight. I got off the phone and started singing "Great Is Thy Faithfulness" because by now I believed God *could* answer prayer. I wanted to remind myself of His faithfulness, and I hoped He *would* answer my prayer to meet our financial needs. Sure enough, He came through. There was a knock at the door. A neighbor from across the street, whom I did not know, but whose son Bryan played with, asked if she could come in. She stumbled around with her words, and all I thought was that she was going to tell me that Bryan had beat up her son. Oh no, she wanted to tell me that the Lord had spoken to her husband's heart and told him to give us money. She asked if I wanted cash or a check. Well, anyone who wants to give me money can decide how to give it to me. I followed her to her house, where I met her sweet husband, and he wrote a check for $1,000! Boy, do we have a good God!

Another time the Lord showed His faithfulness in such a timely manner was when we had no medical insurance or money to go to a doctor. Our daughter Katie was only two years old, and she was sick. I prayed and reminded the Lord (like He had to be reminded) that He was the Great Physician, and that I needed His help for Katie. Right after that, a neighbor whom, again, I hardly knew, came to the door with his two-year-old daughter and asked if Katie could play with her. I explained that Katie was sick with a terrible cold and with conjunctivitis in her eyes. He said his wife was a doctor and that she just happened to be at home.

He suggested I take Katie to their house so his wife could examine her. The doctor not only examined Katie, but she also gave me sample medications for her, including eye drops. Now that's our good God at work again!

    I could write a whole book just about how God provided for us day in and day out. It was amazing! Yet my life was wrapped around doing good so that God would take care of us. God says, "I have loved you with an everlasting love" (Jeremiah 31:3). He does not love us because of what we do, but because of who we are: His children. It was during this time that I added a judgmental spirit to my legalistic lifestyle. If people suffered, that meant they were not living for the Lord. After all, look how good He had been to me.

    As I continued to "do good," God tried to teach me that suffering is not necessarily the result of sin. Jesus said, "Neither this man nor his parents sinned, but this happened so that the works of God might be displayed in him" (John 9:3). I knew that verse and yet, rather than taking God at His word, I patted myself on my back for all my good works. Fortunately, we have a loving and merciful God who is long-suffering. He knew the day would come when I would be eager for Him to teach me more about His character and the freedom He offers through Christ.

CHAPTER 4
A NEW CHAPTER OF MY LIFE

After Lynn married, Ty went away to college, and Katie and Bryan were in middle and high school. At that time, the Lord opened a door for me to volunteer on a congressional political campaign. Around the same time, I met the mother of an eleven-year-old boy who attended our church. I always liked meeting the parents of the children I taught at church. During my home visit, I learned that his mother had no confidence in herself, and that she survived on welfare checks. She wasn't disabled, but she had no incentive to find a job. It wasn't long after meeting her that I met a candidate who was running for Congress, and he talked about a welfare reform bill that he promised to pass if he were elected.

It would require parents currently collecting welfare benefits, and who were physically able, to get a job or go to school in order to continue receiving many of their benefits. This bill, after becoming law, would encourage my friend to make something of herself. After all, she was smart but had no self-esteem. I decided I would do my part to help get the candidate elected so he could do his part to get the bill passed. I volunteered on his campaign, and after a long hard battle, he was elected by 68 percent of the vote. He was instrumental in getting the welfare bill passed, and my friend ended up getting a job and going to school. She also recognized that God was her strength. Once elected, the congressman offered me a job in his local district office.

Since two of our children were out of the house and the other two didn't need my full-time care, I accepted the job and worked for the congressman for five years until Tyre had his first stroke in January 2000. Tyre traveled with his job, and on that particular day, he was north of Birmingham, Alabama, when he called me to say he couldn't see clearly. I thought it was his glaucoma acting up, so I told him to keep his eye with glaucoma closed and drive home. When he arrived home, he called his eye doctor for an appointment, and after describing his symptoms, he was told to come in immediately. After various tests, the doctor gave us disturbing news: "You have had a stroke. You have lost half your sight in both eyes. Go directly to the hospital."

We were both shocked, and as I drove to the hospital, I wondered, *How can this be? What does this mean for Tyre's future?* The unknown gripped me with fear. When we arrived at the hospital, Tyre was admitted immediately for a stroke. Throughout this entire time, while I fretted, Tyre was calm and knew God had it all under control. How I wished I had his faith. I stayed at his side throughout his stay in the hospital, but that didn't stop my office from calling me with questions and problems. Finally, after two months of being pulled between the job that I truly enjoyed and the desire to be with Tyre during his recuperation, I knew my focus had to be with Tyre. I resigned from my job, believing once again that God would provide for our needs, which, once again, He was faithful to do.

Later that same year, a candidate for sheriff asked me to run his campaign with the help of a friend who I had worked with on the congressional campaign. Again, the excitement of a campaign sent my adrenaline through the roof. Tyre's eyesight had improved, but he was not permitted to drive yet, so he was the volunteer campaign photographer and my sidekick. We had a great time, and, once again, our candidate was elected.

The Prayer that Changed My Life

By the end of 2000, Tyre had regained his eyesight. He was permitted to drive, and was back on the road, selling security equipment, while I worked for the newly elected sheriff as a project manager. Life was finally back to normal.

In 2004, Tyre went in for a routine checkup, and the doctor recommended that he have a heart catheterization due to symptoms he had described to the doctor. We were both in shock once again when the doctor told us Tyre had five blocked arteries and needed bypass surgery immediately. Fortunately, he recovered quickly from the surgery, but six weeks later, he had another stroke. Again, it happened while he was traveling. He stopped at a rest stop, called me, and said he didn't feel well.

I asked, "Do you feel like you can make it home, or should I come get you?"

He assured me he felt like he could make it home. God's hand was upon him, because by the time he arrived home, I could barely understand him. I immediately thought, *Please, Lord, not another stroke!* We went directly to the hospital, where again he was admitted. By morning, he had totally lost his speech, and his entire right side was paralyzed. Although I was devastated, there was never any doubt in Tyre's mind that God would help him recover. He told me many times, the best he could, "God will help me." Once again, I wished I had the relationship with God that Tyre had. It took two years for Tyre to recover, but he never complained about his situation. Rather, he used his physical challenges to encourage others.

After Tyre recovered, he met a man in a wheelchair who had also had had a stroke. They discovered that the effects of their strokes were similar. The man could not believe that Tyre walked and talked so well. Tyre explained that he worked hard and every day asked for God's help. He then told him that after he'd learned to walk again, he'd walked a 5K for the American Heart Association. The man got so excited at the thought of the possibility of walking again that he decided to follow in Tyre's footsteps by working hard to learn to walk. Each time the man saw Tyre, he told him how far he'd walked that week. The following year, Tyre took a picture of the man pushing his wheelchair over a 5K finish line. Tyre trusted the Lord so completely that no matter the circumstance, he stayed positive, and his attitude spilled over to others—including me.

When Tyre returned to work in 2006, he was assigned a job selling new products. This was not where his heart was, so he decided to find another job. I also felt that it was time for me to leave my job at the sheriff's office. By now, Lynn, Ty, and Bryan were out of the house, and Katie was still living with us, but was on her own. In February 2007, after much prayer, we felt the Lord leading us to St. Augustine, Florida, to help our daughter Lynn and our son-in-law, Joel, build their home health care business. St. Augustine had always been part of their territory, but they didn't have time to serve it. Since Tyre and I enjoyed working with people, we looked forward to serving our new community. It was our job to hire caregivers to help the elderly in their homes. We enjoyed signing up new clients and hiring caregivers to care for them. Unfortunately, my tender heart overshadowed good business sense, and when caregivers called out at the last minute, I handled the cases myself. Within four months, I was burned out, and I knew the home health care business was not for me. Tyre continued as the marketing person, while the home office in Palm Coast took over the clients in St. Augustine until Joel found a new staff member to take my place.

The day I quit that job, I received a letter from a friend in Pensacola who indicated he had been appointed by the governor to be the director of a new state agency. He hired me and three others to get the agency up and running. Right then, I was reminded, "For my thoughts are not your thoughts, neither are your ways my ways" (Isaiah 55:8). I thought we'd moved to St. Augustine to work in home health care, but God simply used that to get us in the area for me to help start a new state agency. God knew that if He had told me, "I'm sending you to St. Augustine to start a state agency from scratch," I would not have accepted it as being from God. After all, what did I know about such a monumental task?

Today as I look back, I am simply amazed at the opportunities the Lord has given me over the years. As I have learned, God doesn't need our abilities, but He wants our availability. Another one of His promises is "Call to me and I will answer you and tell you great and unsearchable things you do not know" (Jeremiah 33:3). He certainly has done that!

While my faith had continued to grow in certain areas of my life, fear often gripped my heart, and I wondered what would happen if tragedy struck our family. I tried to think of every possible hardship that could come my way and come up with solutions so I would not be caught off guard. I never had peace, because I still did not have a relationship with God where I trusted Him no matter what came my way. Although I did not realize it at the time, through my jobs, God has taught me that I can do all things through Him because He gives me what I need to get the job done. After all, what did I know about running a congressional office, or being the lead person at the sheriff's office to build an eight-million-dollar addition to the office? My job for many years was being a homemaker, not part of the working world, but God equipped me to do these jobs. During this time, I strived to do right to please God, but there were times where I knew I had failed Him by putting my job before my family. I rationalized it by saying my kids were teenagers and didn't need me at home. Once, Katie asked me why I spent more time at work than at home. I can still see Tyre's sad eyes when I told him again and again that I couldn't do what I'd promised because I had to be with my boss at another event. During those times, rather than asking for forgiveness, correcting the issue, and moving on, I beat myself up because I was sure God did not want to hear from me. That was simply a lie of the devil. God waited for me to return to Him. He kept saying, "Call on Me. Draw near to Me." Although I stepped away from Him, He never left me!

Finally, one day when Tyre and I had one of our after-work cups of coffee on the lanai and talked about my day at work, I realized my passion for my job had overshadowed everything else in my life, and that I needed to prioritize what was most important. The first thing I did was to not allow anything to get in the way of my devotions each morning. It was when I spent time with the Lord and got direction and strength for the day. This included when I went on trips with my job. I kept a Bible in my suitcase so that I never had an excuse to not read God's Word. When I was home, Tyre and I had devotions and prayed each morning before I left for work.

Tyre was my biggest cheerleader, but he kept me balanced so that I kept my priorities intact. He sent me texts just to say he loved me, or reminded me ahead of time if we had a commitment so that I'd be home on time. When I was upset about something, Tyre always had a way of fixing everything, so while I was having daily devotions and prayer time, I continued to depend more on Tyre than on God to direct my path.

Psalm 27:14 tells us to wait for the Lord, not your husband. Entwine yourself around the Lord. He is the One who gives peace when our eyes remain on Him. I understand God gives us our husbands. We are to be as one, but God is to be number one in everyone's lives. I loved God, but I loved and depended on Tyre more.

CHAPTER 5

MY PRAYER

Two thousand fourteen was one of the best years of our lives. It started in January when Tyre and I decided to rent a cabin in the mountains of Tennessee for our entire family of nineteen during the Christmas holidays. I found the perfect eight-bedroom cabin on top of a mountain overlooking Gatlinburg, Tennessee. It was perfect! At the end of January, I contacted Lynn, Ty, Bryan, and Katie to get their commitments to meet at the cabin the day after Christmas and stay through New Year's Day. Since Tyre and I had paid for the cabin, I received four quick confirmations that they and their families would attend our family reunion. Family has always been so important to Tyre and me, so we looked forward all year to this special time when we would all be together.

The Prayer that Changed My Life

Two thousand fourteen was also our Disney year because we spent so much time enjoying Disney everything! We bought annual passes and went to the parks throughout the year. Some highlights were in February when we went to the outstanding flower show at Epcot. In September we went on the most amazing Disney cruise with Lynn, Joel, and their two youngest children, Madison and Joshua. For our forty-sixth anniversary in November, we went to Disney and stayed on Disney property. The people treated us like royalty, with gifts and discounts. We bought a Disney art print of Minnie and Mickey gazing into each other's eyes with huge smiles. Tyre and I agreed that that could have been us. We loved each other so much. Life continued to be good!

More good news came in December when Tyre was told he could go from part-time to full-time with full benefits at the St. Johns County tax collector office starting in January. This was a real blessing to get more hours and benefits for doing something he simply loved. After receiving the news, together we prayed and asked God to show us if it made sense for me to resign from my state job to be home when Tyre came home from work. For seven years, he had been so patient with me and had taken on the homemaking and financial responsibilities while my job took me away from home many days at a time. And when I wasn't traveling, my home base was Jacksonville, so I was still traveling at least an hour to and from work each day. Each night when I came home from driving in heavy traffic, he was there with the coffee made and his quiet spirit ready to listen as I voiced all my frustrations. He seldom said anything until I finally took a breath, and then he would say, "You're home now. Enjoy your time with me." And I did, each and every day. After much prayer, I gave my resignation letter effective March 20, 2015.

Life was so good that year, but the best days for both of us were in December when we spent an entire week with our kids, grandkids, and great-granddaughter in Tennessee. Each family took a day to prepare an amazing meal. The cabin was so big that the adults could get together on one floor to talk and reminisce while the kids played pool and other games provided on one of the other two floors. It is hard to believe, but even with nineteen people, many being young children, there were no fights or arguments. God's favor was on all of us. What a blessing it was for our entire family to enter the new year together. Could life be any better? God had been so gracious to us throughout our lives, but especially in 2014 when Tyre and I spent so many quality days together and with our family members.

We entered 2015 on a high. When we returned home from Tennessee, my heart overflowed with gratitude for everything that the Lord had blessed us with. One morning in January during my devotions, I talked with the Lord and thanked Him for His love and goodness to us. Then I said, "Lord, last year was so amazing. You just showered us with so many blessings. I don't ever want to take You for granted and think of You as my Santa Claus. There are so many people hurting in this world, and it doesn't make sense to me. You love them as much as you love me, so why do they have to suffer so much? *Lord, I want to get to know You better so that I really understand who You are.* Now understand, Lord, I'm not asking You to bring suffering into my life to teach me who You are. And above all, if You take Tyre away from me, I want You to know that You will have a crazy woman on Your hands." I meant that last sentence with all my heart; it was not a joke! Tyre had been my rock, my provider, my helper, my source of comfort, my counselor, and my defender. Without him, I felt I would be good for nothing; however, in my heart I truly wanted to know God better.

CHAPTER 6

Satan Tried to Defeat, but God Showed His Love

Tyre loved his full-time job. It meant he was able to help people more in the office. I counted the days until I could once again be a homemaker and make coffee for Tyre when he came home, and unlike when I had complained about my day, he would tell me all about the *good* things that had happened during his day. He was so positive; I guess that is one reason why people loved being around him.

One afternoon as we were outside drinking our coffee, the discussion came up about whether I would be happy staying at home when I quit my job. After all, I had been working some high-stress jobs, so going from that to wondering which

The Prayer that Changed My Life

recipe to make for supper did not sound like much of a challenge for me. After talking about some possible options, politics came into the discussion. I always loved running political campaigns, so maybe it made sense for me to attend classes to find out the latest and greatest winning strategies. We agreed I would look into taking classes.

I found a one-day political campaign class in Orlando, so we both attended. After Tyre saw the excitement in my eyes, he knew this was exactly what I needed to do, so I signed up for the extensive classes in Orlando. Life continued on track with the goodness of God. Tyre was thrilled with his job, and I was excited about returning to my heart's desire: running campaigns. I had friends who asked me to run various campaigns, so I knew once I learned the latest in the digital world of campaigns, I could hit the ground running. I had already talked with others who had agreed to join my campaign teams. Tyre was looking forward to being my photographer as he had been with every campaign I managed. We were ready to get back into the hectic challenges of winning more elections.

On March 17, Tyre was on his way back to his office, unloading his car of boxes from various offices, and as he picked up a box and turned around, his foot caught on the dolly. He tripped and fell straight back, hitting his head. By the time the rescue personnel arrived, he was sitting up. Other than a slight headache, he felt fine, but they recommended that he go to the hospital to be checked out. I received a call from his office saying he had fallen and hit his head, but that he was alert and was being transported to the hospital. They suggested I meet him there.

As I drove the hour drive from Jacksonville to St. Augustine, I talked with the Lord and said, "Lord, as I have told You many times, I need Tyre. He is my everything. I told You that if You take him, You will have a crazy lady on Your hands, and I mean it. Please take care of him. Give the doctors wisdom as they treat him, and Lord, I need peace. Please help me not to fall apart when I see him."

Since he had been transported to the hospital by ambulance, I had it in my head that he wasn't all right, so I tried to prepare myself for the worst by saying things like, "I need to be strong for Tyre if he isn't doing good." And yet I didn't know what I would do if he wasn't well. When I arrived at the hospital, Tyre was sitting up with a worried look on his face, but as soon as our eyes met, a look of relief came over him. He was so happy to see me, and I was so relieved to see how alert he was. How thankful we were when the doctor told us that the CAT scan looked good and we could go home.

That Friday, March 20, Tyre returned to the doctor to get the approval to return to work the following Monday. That same day was bittersweet as I packed up my office. It had been an opportunity of a lifetime to help start a new state agency, but now it was time to move on. I was excited to think that the next day, I would be starting back in the political world.

We spent Friday night in Orlando, and the next morning Tyre took me to the campaign class and then went back to the hotel. He made friends with the manager and was able to get a good deal on a hotel room rate for the future seminars I would be attending. He sat by the pool. Life was good.

That evening, Tyre said he had a headache, but we brushed it off as him not eating lunch, so we stopped to eat on our way to St. Petersburg, where we would watch our grandson perform in a play. On our way back to the hotel, Tyre said he felt somewhat better. We crawled into bed, kissed, and said the same "I love you" that we had said every night for over forty-six years. At 1:00 a.m., I was awakened by the bed shaking. Tyre was half on the bed and half off. I tried to help him get back on the bed, but he was dead weight. I called 911, thinking he'd had another stroke. They told me to lay him on the floor, then instructed me to ask him to respond to various questions. His words were slurred, so

I was convinced he'd had another stroke. By the time rescue personnel arrived, he was on the floor, unconscious and with a foamlike substance coming out of his mouth.

The EMT asked me what had happened, and I said, "He fell and bumped his head on Tuesday, but the doctor gave him a clean bill of health yesterday. He had two strokes over ten years ago, but I think he's had another one." His symptoms indicated to me that he was having another stroke, so I thought it was important to relay that to the EMTs. They asked me what hospital they should take him to, but I didn't know anything about Orlando, so I said, "Take him to the best hospital for strokes."

Two EMTs took Tyre to the ambulance, and the third one walked me to my car, put the address of the hospital in my GPS, wrote down the address, and told me not to try to follow them. Here I was, by myself in a huge city, driving on lonely streets, not knowing where I was headed, and crying out to God, saying, "Please help Tyre. I need him. Lord, help me. God, I need You more than ever. Help me to be strong for Tyre."

I drove up to the emergency room entrance of the hospital, and a police officer came to my car window and asked what I wanted. I said, "My husband was brought here. He's had a stroke."

The Prayer that Changed My Life

He asked, "By ambulance? No ambulance has come here, and you can't get in through the emergency room."

I showed the officer the piece of paper with the hospital address and asked, "Is this the right hospital?"

He acknowledged that it was, and I burst into tears. Seeing how distraught I was, he told me to talk to his supervisor, who was standing at the end of the building. I drove to the end of the building, and the officer walked up to my window. Seeing me in tears, he asked how he could help me. Between sobs, I said, "I have to get to my husband, who was brought to the emergency room."

The officer was so compassionate, and he told me I could get into the hospital by going to the front of the building. He directed me to go around to the parking garage, and then I would see the front of the hospital. I drove around and came to a parking garage, but I couldn't see the front of the building. As I sat in the middle of the road, wondering where to go, God sent me help. The hospital security guard drove up next to me and said, "Follow me." I guess the police officer had told him to make sure I found my way. He took me to the front of the building and walked me into the hospital. He told the guard inside that I was looking for my husband, and that he was supposed to be in the emergency room. The guard dialed the ER number and handed me the phone.

I said, "I'm looking for my husband. Is Tyre Weaver back there?"

There was a pause, and then I heard, "No."

I burst out crying again and said, "He has to be. The EMT said they brought him here."

Sensing my despair, the person on the other end of the phone said, "Let me check in the back." They soon came back and said that he was back there, but that I couldn't go back until someone came to get me. What I learned later was that they'd had a shooting victim walk into the emergency room, and not knowing if the shooter was behind him, they locked down the ER. The ambulance had taken Tyre in via a different entrance, and he was in the last room of the ER, so none of the police officers or the people answering the phone had seen the ambulance or Tyre being brought in.

I waited for what I thought was an hour, but what was probably only fifteen minutes, praying, "Lord, help Tyre right now, and please, can You give me strength to be strong for Tyre? I need You, Lord." The hospital chaplain came and escorted me back to Tyre's room. I went in and again broke down when I saw him lying unconscious and hooked up to a breathing machine, with IVs in both arms. This hadn't happened when he'd had his strokes.

I asked, "What's wrong with him? Why does he have the tube down his throat?"

The chaplain, sensing my despair, said, "The doctor will be in to talk to you in just a few minutes."

I stared at Tyre, and then I began kissing his head and his hand while assuring him, "Everything will be okay." The chaplain was so kind as I cried. I know he was trying to distract me by asking me about Tyre and how long we had been married, but all I could say was, "He is my best friend in the whole wide world."

About ten minutes later, a tech came into the room to do a procedure, and asked me and the chaplain to step out of the room. By now, I felt like I would collapse, so I leaned against the wall for stability as I cried and continued to tell the chaplain how much I loved Tyre and that we were best friends who did everything together. It wasn't longer than a few minutes before the chaplain introduced me to the emergency room doctor. She also showed so much compassion by asking about Tyre and how long we had been married. Then she told me, "I noticed that your husband has a bump on his head. How did that happen?"

I explained, "He fell, but the doctor gave him a clean bill of health."

Her words took me off guard when she said, "Your husband had a brain bleed. Blood has pushed his brain to the left side of his skull. He has to have surgery, but it can't be done until we reverse the blood-thinning medicine. It will take a couple of hours. Does he have a DNR?"

The wind was knocked out of me. At one point, I thought I would faint or throw up. I thought, *Why would she ask me if he has a DNR? Surely he isn't going to die. God wouldn't allow that to happen. I need Tyre.* Taking a deep breath, I replied, "Yes," and explained that three weeks earlier we had had a trust drawn up, and we'd both agreed at that time that we wanted to go to be with Jesus if something happened and we didn't have quality of life. I then said to the doctor, "Please take good care of him, because he is my best friend in the whole wide world."

The doctor assured me that they would do their best, and she left. I knew I had to be strong for Tyre, so I stopped crying before the chaplain and I went back into Tyre's room. I held Tyre's hand as I told the chaplain everything was going to be all right. We loved the Lord, and He would take care of Tyre. The chaplain only left my side for a few minutes the entire three hours we were in the emergency room. At one point when it was obvious that Tyre's hospital stay would be lengthy, the chaplain asked where I planned to stay while

The Prayer that Changed My Life

Tyre was in the hospital. I told him I had no clue. The GPS had gotten me to the hospital, and that was the extent of me knowing where I was in Orlando. All I knew about Orlando was how to get to Walt Disney World, SeaWorld, and the malls. Other than that, I knew nothing about the city. He told me about a local hospitality house, the Hubbard House, which was similar to a Ronald McDonald House and was associated with the hospital. He offered to make a reservation for me to stay there while Tyre recovered. Another blessing from the Lord!

I often said Tyre reminded me of Jesus because He was so kind, giving, and unconditionally loving. He taught me many lessons in his quiet ways. As I watched the medicine drip into his veins, I thought about all he had taught me about persevering through the obstacles of life. In times when we'd had no income, he'd assured me that God would provide because we had done everything we could do to provide for our family. And sure enough, God was faithful to provide our needs. In times when my jobs were stressful, he encouraged me to persevere by reminding me, "I can do all things through Christ." In times when he'd lost his job, he had peace knowing God would provide something else for him, and He did. He always had peace no matter the circumstances. Months after his second stroke, I found a paper on which he had written with his left hand (because the right side of his body was paralyzed), "Today I will do my best to do everything I can to write better, walk better, talk better, and do everything I can do better, and give God all the glory!" He lived every day of his life to please the Lord. He taught me that when I find myself in a storm, I should keep moving forward. I learned this lesson once when we were on the interstate and it started raining so hard, we had to slow to a crawl. People all around us had pulled over to the side of the road. I asked Tyre if he thought we should pull over, and he said, "You will never get through the storm if you don't keep moving forward." How true this is in whatever storm of life we face. Sitting in the storm of self-pity will never get you out of it. It's up to you to keep moving forward. Sitting with him in the hospital in Orlando, remembering his faith and strength in the Lord, was a testing time for me. I kept thinking about how God had healed him in the past, so I knew He could do it again. But would He?

After three long hours, the reversal medicine was finished, and at 5:00 a.m., the doctor told me it was time for surgery. I followed Tyre's stretcher to the doors of the surgery room, then kissed his forehead and told him, "Be strong; you will be fine." Then he was rolled into surgery. The chaplain took me to the waiting room, where I texted the kids to call me when they woke up. I figured they couldn't do anything right then, so they might as well get some sleep. The chaplain prayed with me, and I told him that he could leave and that I would be all right. He had remained with me since I had arrived, and I knew there were others who needed the comfort he had provided me. Sitting alone in the huge, quiet, empty waiting room, I cried out to God, "This is too hard. Be with the doctors. Guide their hands. Give Tyre strength."

Our son Ty was scheduled to run a marathon that morning, so he was already up when he got my text. He called me and told me he was on his way over from St. Petersburg. He was the first to arrive, with his wife, Shannon. She has such a servant's heart, and soon after they arrived she offered to get me coffee or food. I hadn't wanted anything since 4:30 p.m. the day before when we'd stopped to get something to eat when Tyre wasn't feeling well, so by now I was weak. I welcomed a warm cup of coffee, but my stomach was in knots, so I couldn't handle food. Lynn called soon after Ty called, and she and Joel drove over from Palm Coast. Katie's phone was turned off, so she didn't know anything was wrong until she woke up around 10:00 a.m. I tried calling her throughout the morning, until my phone died, and then I used Tyre's phone. She knew something was up when she turned on her phone and saw all the missed calls. She drove over from St. Augustine later that morning. Bryan was in the army, stationed in Arizona. He called early in the morning, and I explained what had happened, then told him I'd call him back after the surgery was over. Those of us in the waiting room made small talk as we anxiously waited for news. I found myself going back and forth to the surgery doors, hoping someone would tell me something. We finally received a call from the surgical room at about 8:00 a.m. saying things were going well.

Our kids loved their dad, or, as Ty called him, "Pop." He would do anything for his kids, like the time Ty's truck broke down in Fort Myers and Tyre drove eight hours from Pensacola to help him get it fixed. He was always texting the kids, telling them he loved them and to have a nice day. That's just the kind of dad he was. Now we waited and wondered what the outcome of the surgery would be. Three long hours later, I was outside the surgery room and the doctor walked out looking weary, but said, "The surgery went well. He is not out of the woods, but he is strong, so he'll make it."

A burden rolled off my shoulders. I ran back to the waiting room with tears of joy in my eyes to tell the kids the good news, and we immediately thanked God for His goodness to us and for healing for Tyre.

The Prayer that Changed My Life

It would be some time before we could see Tyre, so we walked over to the Hubbard House to settle into my home away from home. It was a true blessing: a beautiful private room and three meals a day for a nominal fee, and a precious staff who encouraged all the families of patients in the intensive care unit of the hospital. As I think back, I'm amazed at God's love that was demonstrated over and over throughout the three weeks we were in Orlando through the people at the Hubbard House. We even received visits from others from local churches who I didn't know but who came and prayed with me on a daily basis while I sat at Tyre's side, waiting for any improvement.

After eating a meal provided by the Hubbard House staff, it was time to return to the hospital. We walked into Tyre's ICU room and I broke down crying, seeing his head wrapped in gauze, hearing the sound of the breathing machine, and seeing tubes coming out of his neck and the IVs in his arms. His eyes were closed, and he appeared to be sleeping comfortably. Ty held his hand and said, "Pop, squeeze my hand."

We probably made way too much noise for the ICU, but we were so ecstatic when Tyre squeezed his hand. Then it was my turn. It was the best feeling to feel that ever-so-slight squeeze. We told him to move his toes, and he did with gusto! Praise God; Tyre had heard us and responded. He would be fine! Finally we could relax!

Over the next three weeks, Bryan was able to get leave from the army to stay with me for a week. Lynn was there most days, and Katie and Ty came as their jobs permitted. Grandkids came to be with me, which was a real treat because they were a big distraction for me, talking about the latest video games or about what was happening in school. My sister, Kim, came from Massachusetts and stayed for a week. She brought such comfort with her funny antics, which helped relieve the stress that I faced each day. Together we claimed verses for healing. There was no doubt that God would answer our prayers. After all, for years He had been so good, so we believed He would bring healing because we claimed healing verses and had faith that God would honor us for our faith.

Tyre's brother, Bob, Bob's wife, and their two sisters, Kim and Connie, surprised me by coming down from Alabama and Georgia. Our pastor came twice a week from St. Augustine, and he often said, "Father knows best." Those words would ring loud and clear in the weeks and months down the road, but at that point I agreed that Father knows best. And since the best was having Tyre with me, I was convinced that Tyre would be healed.

Evenings were the toughest. I was exhausted sitting by Tyre's side all day every day, but I was never too tired to hold his hand and pray, asking God to give him a good night's rest. Then I would give him a kiss, walk back to my room, and cry as the "what if" questions took over my thought process. *What if he doesn't make it? What if he doesn't get back to his normal self?* I tried to prepare myself for the worst, but I hoped for the best. After I cried buckets of tears, I put on praise music on my iPad because through the years when I would get discouraged, it was music that was a soothing balm to my weary body.

For three long roller-coaster weeks, my family and I clung to God's promises, believing that Tyre would walk out of the hospital. I went to the hospital each morning at 10:00 a.m., the beginning of visiting hours. Although Tyre was on a breathing machine and always looked like he was sleeping, I talked to him and read him cards that people had sent. I put my iPad on his pillow and played hymns that he loved. Although he'd stopped squeezing our hands days before, he always moved his feet at our commands, so I knew he could hear me.

Tyre had such wonderful, compassionate nurses. Each morning they spent time with me, telling me what kind of night he'd had; sometimes he'd had good nights, and other nights he was fidgety. Since Tyre was on heavy medication and had a breathing tube, the nurses couldn't get to know Tyre, so they asked me about his personality. I told them he was kind and quiet. I asked one nurse, Sarah, if patients ever returned so she could meet them, and she said yes. I told her I couldn't wait for her to meet the real Tyre without all the tubes. She said she looked forward to that day.

After ten days on the breathing tube, the doctor decided to replace it with a tracheostomy. I was so excited to see him without the breathing tube. He looked so much more normal now that he didn't have the tube in his throat. I was so hopeful that he would wake up, but he didn't. Thinking it was the heavy pain medicines that were keeping him asleep, I asked the doctor if he would lower the dosage, but lowering the medication made him fidgety because he was in so much pain, so they had to increase them again. Finally, the day came when his vitals were stable; he was released from the ICU to the step-down unit, but he still was not awake. We rejoiced that he must be getting better if he had been released from the ICU. I slept well that night, thinking we were on the road to recovery.

Disappointment set in the next day when I arrived and the nurse told me an infection had set in, and that he had taken a turn for the worse. Back to the ICU! How could this be? He'd been doing so well. I had more tears, more questions. "Why God? What's going on? I can't handle this. Help me, Lord." It was determined that the infection wasn't as bad as they'd originally thought, but because his vitals were unstable, he had to stay in the ICU. That was fine with me because that is where he had progressed.

Then there was more bad news. An EEG (test of the brain) was performed, and it showed he was having many seizures, so more medicines were given to try to stop them.

Doctors often made rounds at night, so if the nurse told me the doctors were coming, I stayed in Tyre's room, even if it was after regular visiting hours. I wanted to get the latest news on Tyre's condition. Since seizures of the brain don't necessarily show outward appearances, I didn't know if the new medicines were working or not.

On the evening of April 11, 2015, while visiting with Tyre and waiting for the doctor to arrive, I was on the bench at the end of his bed, reading my emails. The doctor and nurse came into the room and, with no emotion in her voice or in her expression, the doctor looked at me and said, "Tyre is brain-dead. You said when he first came into the hospital that he wouldn't want to be kept alive if he didn't have quality of life." She went on to explain in medical terms what was going on in his brain, and that he was at the bottom of the scale of some test.

All I heard was "brain-dead." Nothing else registered with me. I felt like I had been hit in the gut by a wrecking ball, or as if the doctor's scalpel had just ripped out my heart. I looked at both of them in disbelief. Immediately I thought, *How can this be? God was supposed to heal him. After all, my heavenly Father knows I need Tyre. If this is true, then, God, You have a crazy lady on Your hands. You aren't who You said You are—a loving and faithful God.*

As those thoughts rushed through my mind, I couldn't speak. I just walked out of the room. My breath was sucked out of me; I didn't know what to do or where to go. I ended up downstairs in the lobby, calling Lynn to tell her the news.

Then I called my sister, Kim, and said, "Tyre is brain-dead! Where is your God now?"

She replied, "I don't know."

She later told me she didn't know what to say. I screamed things that I don't remember, but it was as much of a shock to her as it was to me—both the news of Tyre's condition and my reaction.

I was so angry. What had happened to the good God I'd told everyone about? He sure wasn't being good now! I roamed the hospital, crying, and then went back to the ICU.

The Prayer that Changed My Life

As I waited to be buzzed into the unit, I had tears running down my face, and a lady in the waiting room hugged me. I don't know who she was, but I am convinced the Lord sent her to give me a hug from Him to show me He loved me and understood my heartache.

I went back into Tyre's room and looked at the nurse, who was standing at the foot of his bed, staring at him. "Is he *really* brain-dead?" I asked.

She shook her head yes and continued to stare at him. I walked up to the side of his bed, kissed him over and over, and told him I loved him, then walked out of the hospital. Crying uncontrollably, I had to get outside to get some air. I felt like I was suffocating. I walked around the property of the hospital and ended up, at 11:30 p.m., on a park bench on the corner of the street of the Hubbard House. A man walked by, then came back and asked, "Is your family looking for you?"

I shrugged my shoulders because I did not know, nor did I care.

A little while later, I saw Lynn and Joel walking toward me as I sat on the bench. "How did you find me?" I asked, confused.

"A man came to the hospital and told us you were here. You don't know him?"

"No," I replied. "Did you?"

"No," said Lynn.

We were both convinced it had to have been an angel. We never saw the man again.

As I stared off into space, Lynn said something like, "We have to trust God, Mom." Those words stung beyond belief! I quickly said, "He may be your God, but He isn't mine."

I got up and walked toward the Hubbard House, leaving my poor daughter crying her heart out. What had happened to the mother who'd quoted verses to her, who'd said she trusted God, who'd said God was so good?

As I entered my room, I thought, *What am I saying? If I don't have God, I have nothing.* It was like reality struck me. Who was I to expect God to do what I thought He should do? Father may know best, but right then I also knew He had His hands full with a woman who leaned so heavily on her husband for everything, loved him so dearly, and was totally lost without him.

I got on my knees and said, "Dear God, I hurt so bad right now. I am so sorry for turning my back on You. You are all I have and all I need right now. As I have told You over and over, without Tyre, You have a crazy woman on Your hands because I don't know what to do. Help me, Lord."

In my heart I heard, "My ways are not your ways. My ways are so much bigger." Although the void in my heart was huge, I sensed that God knew what He was doing. I just

The Prayer that Changed My Life

wasn't sure what I was supposed to do without Tyre. I cried myself to sleep.

The next morning, I went to Tyre's room and the doctor came in and asked me what I wanted to do. My choices were to turn off all the machines, take out the IVs, and let Tyre go to heaven naturally, or to allow him to remain on the ventilator, with machines monitoring his vitals and heavy medications, and to live his life out in a nursing home. But being brain-dead, he wouldn't have any quality of life. I knew he wouldn't want to be kept alive by machines and medicines. I would be selfish to keep him from going to be with Jesus.

I asked, "How long will he live without the machines?"

The doctor said, "Maybe a day or two, and then his organs will start shutting down. We will give him medicine to keep him comfortable."

An unexplainable peace came over me. That meant we could have time with Tyre without all the noises of the machines, and he would be relaxed, no longer being poked and prodded. With tears in my eyes as I held his hand, they turned off the machines. The quietness in the room was so peaceful. I kissed him and told him how much I loved him. He breathed on his own and looked like he was enjoying some good rest. He was moved to a private room where we could spend time with him. The following day, Bryan flew in from

Arizona, and Lynn, Joel, Ty, Shannon, and Katie joined me at the hospital. We spent the entire day with Tyre, listening to music and thanking God for the time we'd had with him. That night, Bryan and I went to a local hotel, and everyone else went home.

The next morning, April 13, the doctor called me to say that Tyre had died. I asked her if she could keep his body there until we got there. I just had to see for myself that God had promoted him to heaven. She agreed, and I hung up. Bryan and I held each other and cried, knowing how much we would miss him, but we felt relieved that he was with Jesus and in no more pain. When we arrived at the hospital, we saw that all color had left his face, and I knew he was with Jesus. Again, Bryan and I held each other and cried. There was such a huge void in our hearts. It hurt so much.

The nurse came in and asked if we would like chairs in his room for all the family so we could spend time with him. I assured her he was not there; he was healed and spending his day with Jesus in heaven. The body in the bed was simply his shell. I felt sorry for her because she was a new nurse, and appeared to feel awkward being with the family of someone who had just died. She told me that, before Tyre, she had never been with someone when they'd died. She told me she'd held his hand, and he'd appeared to be in pain, so she'd gone to get medicine. When she'd returned a minute later, he was already gone. I hugged her and thanked her for her goodness to Tyre, and we left the hospital.

CHAPTER 7

THE ANSWER TO MY PRAYER

As my son Bryan drove me home from the hospital, all I could say was, "What am I going to do?" I walked into my own home and felt so lost. I didn't know what to do about anything! I had no idea what bills to pay. I'd left the hospital one day to go home to get clothes, and I'd seen a man cutting our lawn. I asked him who he was and if we owed him money. Tyre had always taken care of our finances. What if something broke in the house? What if my car broke down? What if I couldn't pay the bills? The "what ifs" continued to plague me.

After we finished Tyre's memorial service and everyone went home, I sat alone in a chair in my bedroom, staring out the window and crying out to God, "God, what am I going to do? I told You that if You took Tyre from me, You'd have a crazy woman on Your hands, and now here I sit before You with more questions than answers. My credit card was cut off because it was in Tyre's name. I don't have enough money to pay the bills. I hate this house, knowing that two dear people are no longer here—first my mother died, and now Tyre. The silence in the house is deafening. Lord, I need You now more than ever."

Although I knew I needed Him, it took me a month before I could talk with God about the greatest loss of my life. Up until that time, my mind was so fuzzy. I couldn't think straight, nor could I stand staying home in such a lonely house, so I went shopping just to do something. I brought home bags of stuff because they made me feel happy for the moment, but once I arrived home, I left them on the counter for weeks, never looking at them until I decided it was time to clean off the counter. Sleep was almost nonexistent. It is said that grief can cause you to think you are crazy, and I certainly can testify to that. I was never taught how to deal with grief, and now here it was, consuming my life.

I was so exhausted from crying, from my heart aching, and from wondering what had gone wrong. Finally, one day as I was sitting in my chair in my bedroom, I cried out to God, "Why didn't You heal Tyre? You said in Your Word that You will reward them with a long life. You said that whatever I ask, believing in You will do it." I'd had so much faith that I'd planned a reunion with all his nurses when Tyre would walk in and thank them for caring for him.

Again, in my heart, I heard the Lord say, "My ways are not your ways." I may have quoted healing Bible verses, but the Lord showed me that I'd prayed them for my happiness. I'd wanted Tyre to get better and be by my side like he had been for over forty-six years. Sure, I would have given God glory, but my eyes were fixed on healing the love of my life first, and then I would give God glory. He wants us to glorify Him *in the midst* of our trials, and we do that by trusting Him, not turning *from* Him. I have learned through this experience that what we think is a no to our prayers is actually God wanting to do something better if we will have an attitude of gratitude, knowing He makes no mistakes, and that we can trust Him to do what is best for us. Is that hard to do? At first it was very hard, and I must admit I failed Him, but I have learned by spending time in His Word and in prayer, and seeking His perfect will, that He is a merciful God. He will lead me through all storms of life if my focus stays on Him and not on my circumstances around me.

Although I knew in my heart that God makes no mistakes, my mind and heart couldn't accept it. My loving God kept reminding me, "My ways are not your ways," and, "The secret things belong to the LORD our God, but the things revealed belong to us" (Deuteronomy 29:29). He reminded me of my life verses that He had given me in the 1980s when Tyre quit his job and we'd had to trust God to meet our needs: "Trust in the LORD with all your heart and lean not on your own understanding; in all your ways submit to him, and he will make your paths straight" (Proverbs 3:5–6). I had claimed these verses many times over the years, but now it was different. It was as if God Himself had told me to trust Him and not try to figure it out. It was my job to keep my eyes on Him, and He would show me the path He had for me. But in the meantime, I could have peace knowing that Tyre was safe in the arms of Jesus, and that I would see him again.

Looking back, I see how God's love and mercy were so evident throughout the toughest time of my life. I think about the pastor of an Orlando megachurch and his deacons, who we did not know, but who had heard about Tyre and came to the hospital to get on their knees and pray for Tyre and me. God used them to give me His strength to go on. I'm reminded that less than three weeks before Tyre's accident, we had talked about our wishes for when we died or had no quality of life, so I had God's peace with the decision to turn off the machines. God hugged me through the stranger in the

The Answer to My Prayer

ICU who saw me sobbing. She didn't say a word, but gave me a God-filled, heartwarming hug. I continue to be amazed when I think about the man God sent to Lynn and Joel to tell them where I was after being told Tyre was brain-dead. God tells us that there are angels in our midst (Hebrews 13:2), and I truly believe God sent an angel. It was God's way of letting me know He cares for me. His faithfulness was all around me during this agonizing time of my life.

As I think back over those torturous days, I realize now that Satan thought he could use Tyre's accident to defeat me and turn me *from* God, but God used the experience to answer the prayer I had prayed in January: "Lord, I want to get to know You better."

People are always quick to blame God when tragedy strikes, but we are told in God's Word that Satan rules this world for the time being (John 12:31). The good news is that God is still sovereign (in control), and His plans for our lives are not thwarted by anything that happens. He's right here, waiting for us to turn to Him, but as a wise pastor once said, "God is a gentleman, and He will not force Himself on anyone." My prayer kept resounding loud and clear in my head: "Lord, I want to get to know You better." God says in Jeremiah 29:13, "You will seek me and find me when you seek me with all your heart." And that is exactly what I did.

Now my focus was on getting to know God in such a personal way that I would have peace no matter what this world threw at me, and I started with, "God, forgive me for my unbelief. Show me what I need to know to have a deeper relationship with You." When you give God such a request, be ready for answers, because it is His desire to have a personal relationship with His children.

Some people believe we are *all* children of God. The Bible says we are all God's creations (Colossians 1:16), but only those who put their faith and trust in Him are His children (John 1:12). Being a child of God means admitting you are a sinner (Romans 3:23), believing God had His only Son die on the cross for your sins—past, present and future—(Romans 5:8), and confessing to Him that you want Him to come into your life and be your Lord and Savior (Romans 10:13). Remember, He loved you enough to create you, but He will not force you to accept Him as your Savior. But if you do, you will never regret it!

Since Tyre has gone home to heaven, God has become so real to me. He is no longer a God in heaven that I go to when I need something. Mornings are the best time of the day because He talks to me through His Word. I have not only learned about His character, but He is teaching me how to trust Him more and how to walk by faith and not by sight.

The Answer to My Prayer

Each morning, I start out with thanking Him for who He is to me, and then I ask Him to show me something in His Word that will help me to know Him better. I then go to the throne of grace with my questions and requests, knowing He will answer in His timing and in His way.

I know He must laugh at me at times, like the time when I asked Him if I could go to Israel with a local church group. I told Him He would have to provide the money. Two days later, I received a check that I was not expecting, and it was for the amount of the trip. Rather than thanking the Lord, I called my son Ty and asked him if he thought I should use the money for the trip. My wise son asked, "Didn't you ask the Lord for the money?" I am a slow learner, but thankfully I have a patient heavenly Father who knows me well.

CHAPTER 8
LESSONS LEARNED

I was lost during the first nine months after Tyre's exit to heaven. People thought I was doing great, but I was utterly depressed. Life was so different and difficult not having my best friend at my side to make things better. There were no morning kisses, no hearing "I love you," no cup of coffee being handed to me as I got out of bed. Life had become overwhelming. After a couple of months of not knowing which direction to turn to, I decided to try to do five things each day: 1. Get out of bed; 2. Make a cup of coffee; 3. Make up the bed (so I would not get back in it); 4. Spend time with the Lord; and 5. Pick one problem to try to resolve. Note: I said *try* to resolve. Many times it took me days to resolve one problem. Problem solving had always been Tyre's specialty. I didn't have the time or patience to try to solve problems. It was a learning curve for me. I must say, checking off the five things each morning got me into a routine that I later learned was "a new normal," and while I still fought depression, God's gentle nudges helped me to move forward.

One day as I sat in my chair in my bedroom, looking at my bookshelf filled with books, I decided to find a book that would make me feel better. A book about Job nearly jumped off the shelf. I certainly could relate to him—the man who had lost his family, his property, his wealth, and his health. I pulled the book off the shelf, and after reading a few pages, hoping to soak up some sympathy, I realized it was not a "woe is me" book, but rather a book about God's character. It was the beginning of getting to know the one true God who loves me, makes no mistakes, and has a perfect plan for my life. I have learned that God hasn't taken *away from me*, but rather has shown me more of Himself so that I can do the job He has given me to do: glorifying Him. The following are four lessons God taught me about Himself, as of this writing:

LESSON 1: My God is "inscrutable" (Isaiah 40:28).

God being inscrutable means He is impossible to understand. He does not always do the same thing the same way. Just because He *can* heal a body here on earth does not mean He will. Although I cannot understand Him, His character never changes. He is still sovereign, all-knowing, all-powerful, holy, faithful, loving, and perfect in all His ways. If I understood all things about Him, He would simply be like any other human. By focusing on His greatness and His character, which never changes, my "whys" and "what ifs" are no longer my focus.

LESSON 2: My God wants to be my everything.

Where I thought Tyre was my everything, I have learned that my God can meet needs Tyre could never meet. My study of who God is to me revealed the following:

a. Psalm 18:1–2 says my God is my strength, my rock, my fortress, my deliverer, my shield, the horn of my salvation (the horn on an animal is his defense), and my stronghold (a high tower of protection).

b. Isaiah 54:5 says my God is my maker, my husband, and my redeemer. He made me, so He knows me better than I know myself. As my husband, He meets all my needs through His Word and through people. He redeemed me (bought me back) from my sin by His Son paying the price on the cross for my sins. Now that is real love!

c. Psalm 141:8 says my God is my refuge and sovereign Lord. A refuge is a safe place, so I know He will protect me. As my Sovereign Lord, He has everything under control, so there's no need to worry.

d. Romans 15:3 says my God is my hope. This hope is not a "hope so," as in, "I hope He will come through," but rather a "know so," as in having the confidence that what God says is true even though we may not understand it. I have the hope (confidence) that one day I will be in heaven with God even though I have not seen heaven.

e. Psalm 18:18 says my God is my support. When David's enemies confronted him, the Lord was right there supporting him, and since God is no respecter of persons (Romans 2:11), I know He will support me.

f. Psalm 23:1 says my God is my shepherd. A shepherd takes care of his sheep, and when they stray, he lovingly draws them back into the fold. That is exactly what our heavenly Father does with His children. I am so glad that the Lord continued to be my shepherd even when I strayed from Him.

g. Philippians 4:19 says my God is my provider. He promises to provide for all of my needs. While I was out West, He showed me His greatness in the

Teton Range. Looking up at the majestic mountains made me realize just how great He is! If He could put those mountains in place, He certainly can provide for my needs.

h. Hebrews 13:6 says my God is my helper. I have found this to be true on a daily basis. When I cannot figure something out, I simply thank Him for being my helper and wait for Him to show me what to do. I was distraught about landscaping in the front of the house, because when you are selling a house, curb appeal is so important. I cried as I tried to figure out how to dig out dead bushes with a deep root system. I told God I needed help and it wasn't more than five minutes later when a new neighbor walked by and started talking to me. The next thing I knew, he brought another neighbor over, who took care of my problem. God cares about all our problems. What seems monumental to us is nothing for our mighty God to handle.

i. Psalm 73:24 says my God is my guide and my counselor. In order for Him to guide us, we must listen to Him and let Him lead. Out West, my friend and I were on our own, hiking through mountains. After our hike on one particular day, we stopped to eat lunch, and there at the site was a national park guide telling people interesting facts about the area. We'd missed them because we hadn't listened to the guide *before* we'd headed out on our hike. I am learning to wait for my guide to take the first step and not to get ahead of Him. His ways are perfect. He counsels me every morning as I spend time with Him. His counsel has taught me how to trust Him and how to have peace, which I lacked for so long.

j. Romans 15:33 says my God is the God of *peace*. Peace doesn't mean the absence of trials and suffering, but the assurance that God will be right there going through it with me, and He is waiting to hear from me so that He can give me His peace.

k. Second Corinthians 1:3–5 says my God is the God of all comfort. He has used various ways to bring comfort to me:

  i. He comforts me by His presence, which is seen in His creations. I felt His presence when I went out West and looked at the glistening snowcapped mountains and enjoyed the array of wild flowers that created a rainbow of color on the ground. I see His presence in the yellow and orange hues of morning sunrises.

  ii. He comforts me through His Word. In order to discover this comfort, I must spend time with Him. I have a hard time memorizing Scripture, so I write down Bible verses that speak to my heart, and I read them every day during my quiet time with the Lord. It is amazing how often He has brought to mind verses on peace when I find myself going into panic mode. I am learning to quickly refocus on His truths.

iii. He comforts me through Christian music. The Lord reminded me of the story of David playing an instrument when King Saul was not having a good day, and how David's music strengthened the king. There were many days when I could not focus on God's Word. My mind was in a fog. Listening to Christian music ministered to me, with songs reminding me that God doesn't always answer our prayers the way we want Him to, but that we are to trust Him, believing He truly knows best. Another song reminded me that God wants us to lean on Him when our strength is gone, because He is our strength! Today my anthem is "Great Is Thy Faithfulness" because He has been so faithful even when I haven't been faithful to Him. It just makes me love Him more!

iv. God comforts me through my friends. I decided in 2013 that a half marathon might be fun thing to do. Mind you, I have never been involved in any sport except to cheer on athletes, but I decided to give it a try. During my training, when I came home sweating and drained of all energy, the first things I wanted to do was to guzzle down water and to put a cool, wet facecloth on my face and neck to restore my strength. It is much like what my true friends do for me at my weakest moments. When the storms of loneliness and despair come from out of nowhere and I feel like I don't have any energy to continue on, God uses friends to restore my strength through their prayers and encouraging words, and by encouraging me to take walks even when I don't feel like I can put one foot in front of another.

LESSON 3: My God wants me to simply trust Him and be thankful.

Trusting is a moment-by-moment *choice*. It is easy to trust God when things are going well, but what about when the enemies of death, loneliness, depression, and impatience hit like a freight train? I am learning that my inscrutable, all-knowing, all-powerful, all-loving, sovereign God—the one who tells me to give Him all my cares because He cares for me—is big enough to handle every one of my enemies. David in the Bible appeared to be constantly on the run from his enemies, and yet he said, "But I trust in you Lord; I say, 'You are my God. My times are in your hands; deliver me from the hands of my enemies, from those who pursue me'" (Psalm 31:14–15). David understood where his strength and protection came from, and we have the same God wanting to save us from the hands of our enemies, if we will just put our trust in Him.

My life verses, Proverbs 3:5–6, tell me to trust in the Lord with all my heart and not to lean on how I understand things, and if I look to the Lord rather than my situation, He *will*—not maybe—direct all my ways. It is a command, and if we obey the command, there will be no room for despair, worry, or any way for Satan's fiery darts to pierce our shield of faith. Trusting God instead of focusing on myself will bring peace that surpasses all understanding.

For years, I have underlined Bible verses that have spoken to my heart. Recently I found a verse I had underlined at some point of my life: "Do not put your trust in princes, in *human beings*, who cannot save" (Psalm 146:3, emphasis mine). God had warned me years ago not to put my trust in humans, but I did not heed His warning. My trust in God was provisional. I trusted Him if His answer made sense to me; otherwise, I trusted Tyre to work things out for me. After reading the verse, I started to kick myself for not obeying

His command years ago when I'd underlined the verse, but then I read on in verse 9 that the Lord sustains the widows. Immediately, I sensed His love. He did not have to put that verse right there, but He knows me so well. He knew I would be down on myself for not heeding His Word. In other words, my interpretation in what He said is, "Nan, I told you not to put your trust in man, but I understand you are human, and I want you to know that I will sustain you." What love!

When we recognize that God is bigger than any human, can handle *everything* in life, and continues to show us His love, grace, and mercy in all circumstances, then thankfulness and trust will become a way of life.

Thankfulness takes *discipline.* After Tyre's homegoing, my thanksgiving list was limited. As I studied Scripture, I wrote down names that describe who God is to me (Lesson 2). Each morning, I use the list as part of my time of praising my Savior for who He is and all He means to me. It took practice to have an attitude of thanksgiving on a daily basis, because there were many times I woke up feeling discouraged while thinking about everything I had to tackle, but through discipline, it has become a way of life. The Lord is so worthy of our praise! I am so glad I kept it up, because the Lord uses it to help fight my enemies of anxiousness, loneliness, and every other enemy that attacks me when I am least expecting it.

One enemy I fought after Tyre went to heaven was insomnia. When I laid my weary body on my bed, my mind was so charged I could not shut it off. One night when my body was beyond exhaustion and my mind was still fully charged, I told the Lord I had to get some rest and to please shut down my mind. In my heart, I felt the Lord telling me to thank Him for who He is to me. I pulled out of the recesses of my mind the names of God that I had memorized. I thanked Him for being my strength, rock, fortress, deliverer, shield, horn of my salvation, stronghold, maker, husband, redeemer, refuge, sovereign Lord, hope, support, shepherd, provider, helper, guide, counselor, God of peace, and God of all comfort. Then I went through the list again. By the third time, I had drifted off to sleep. Since then, I have continued the practice and, without fail, it works! Ask God who He is to you, then make your list and use it as your insomnia prescription. You will wake up feeling refreshed.

Being thankful changes your mindset. That is why Jesus said, "Give thanks in all circumstances; for this is God's will for you in Christ Jesus" (1 Thessalonians 5:18). Another version says, "In everything give thanks" (NKJV). It is saying that wherever you find yourself, fix your eyes on Jesus and say, "Thank you that *You* have everything under control," because at times like that, it is easy to fix your eyes on the tragedy rather than on the God of the universe, who is never caught off guard.

In 2013, we gave a company a down payment of $20,000 to have our bathrooms and kitchen remodeled and to replace our flooring. The owner of the business went bankrupt and skipped town. Does that mean I am still to thank God? We did not thank God for losing $20,000, but we thanked Him that He had it under control even though we did not understand it. In the fall of 2015, I received a call saying I was being reimbursed for the entire $20,000! It was encouragement that I needed. God knew in 2013 that we did not need the upgrades, we wanted the upgrades. God knew back then that I would need the money in 2015. He is trustworthy, and He is worthy of our praise and thanksgiving no matter the circumstances.

LESSON 4: My God gives peace that passes all understanding.

I had learned so much about my God, but I still did not have peace in my life. I tried to focus on God, but as a human, I got sidetracked and found myself in tears again and again. It was such a roller coaster ride, and while I love roller coasters, I do like to get off them. In February 2016, I read that Jesus said, "Peace I leave with you" (John 14:27). I wrote in my journal, "Not sure how this works. I want peace, but I just don't have it." I told the Lord that I wanted the peace He was talking about. This sent me on a search in God's Word to find out how I could have the peace that God says He gives to His children. As the Lord showed me a verse, I wrote it on an index card. Today I have seven verses that I read each morning because they are as alive today as they were when they were written over two thousand years ago:

- Philippians 4:6–7 (emphasis mine): "Do not be anxious about *anything*, but in every situation, by prayer and petition, *with* thanksgiving, present your requests to God. And the peace of God, which transcends *all* understanding, will guard your hearts and your minds in Christ Jesus."
- Isaiah 26:3 AKJV (emphasis mine): "You [God] will keep him in *perfect* peace, whose mind is stayed (steadfast, unwavering) on you: because he trusts in you."
- 2 Corinthians 10:5b: "We take captive every thought to make it obedient to Christ."
- Romans 8:6b: "The mind governed by the Spirit is life and peace."
- Proverbs 14:30a: "A heart at peace gives life to the body."

- John 14:27: "Peace I leave with you; my peace I give you. I do not give to you as the world gives. Do not let your hearts be troubled and do not be afraid."
- Colossians 3:15: "Let the peace of Christ rule in your hearts."

These are commands, not just suggestions. We are commanded not to worry, but rather to give our requests to God with *thanksgiving*. And when we do, He will give His peace. How does that happen? By remembering that we serve a big God who can and wants to handle our anxieties. After all, He made us and knew we would have anxieties; otherwise, He wouldn't have included that verse in His Word. When we focus on Him and accept His peace, we will have a joyful life rather than having an attitude of "woe is me." Memorize verses or write them on a card, and each morning read them to yourself. Ask God to bring them to mind when you find yourself spending more time worrying than focusing on the God of peace.

I have heard it said, "What gets our attention gets us." If worry gets our attention, it controls us. On the other hand, if our attention is on God, who loves us and wants to provide His best for us, then the peace of God will take over and we will find rest. Another true statement is "Worry is like a rocking chair; it gives you something to do, but it doesn't get you anywhere." God taught me years ago that if you can do something about the problem, do it; otherwise, leave it in God's hands. When you do, stress is replaced with peace.

CHAPTER 9
CONCLUSION

My journey from knowing about God to having a close, personal relationship with God has just begun. Psalm 32:8 says, "I will instruct you and teach you in the way you should go." Teaching takes time. I will never arrive, but I am so excited about what the Lord has taught me thus far. My God came to earth to live among men so that humans with finite minds could see His love and compassion for us and seek after Him. Learning that He is inscrutable (impossible to understand) relieves me of having to try to understand the questions of life. Learning to simply trust in the almighty, all-knowing, all-powerful, sovereign God allows me to have peace during the most troublesome times of life.

The Prayer that Changed My Life

Tyre taught me that every challenge is simply another opportunity in life. We can allow trials, tragedies, and sufferings to get the best of us, or we can use them as opportunities to learn from them and to glorify God while going through them, as Tyre did through all the many challenges of his life. I am so glad God used the challenge in my life as an opportunity to answer my prayer so I could get to know Him better. He did not have to do that, but as I am learning, He does not waste any opportunity to show His character and His unfailing love and grace. It is up to us as to how we respond to the storms of life, but remember, He is there going through it with you.

Who is God to you? Do you keep Him in a box and call on Him during the emergencies of your life? Is He like a good luck charm or *your* Santa Claus? Or do you see Him as your everything—your strength, rock, fortress, deliverer, shield, horn of your salvation, stronghold, husband (if you do not have one), redeemer, refuge, sovereign Lord, hope, support, shepherd, provider, helper, guide, counselor, God of peace, and God of all comfort? I used to spend time thinking of ways to stay on the good side of God. Now I've learned that there is nothing I can do for Him to make Him love me any more or any less. He accepts me as I am. Today I have peace and a burning desire to spend time with Him to seek His perfect will for my life. He says, "Draw nigh to me, and I will draw nigh to you." God used what the world would call a tragedy to change my life. I am so glad religious rituals, legalism, and a judgmental attitude have been replaced with a peace that surpasses all understanding. My God is all that I want and all that I need. He is my everything!

www.ingramcontent.com/pod-product-compliance
Ingram Content Group UK Ltd.
Pitfield, Milton Keynes, MK11 3LW, UK
UKHW022222230426
12048UKWH00016BA/1000